OLLIE YOUNG,

'GREATEST OF ALL

CLUB MANIPULATORS.

Begins Where Others End.

The artistic club juggling of Ollie Young is truly marvelous. The grace and finish with which he handles the clubs is fascinating in the extreme.—*Cincinnati Enquirer, Oct. 3, '99.*

Permanent Address, N. Y. Clipper.

AMERICA AND EUROPE'S

...GREATEST...

JUGGLERS.

EDWARD VAN WYCK.

COMPLIMENTS OF

EDWARD VAN WYCK,

MANUFACTURER OF

High-class Juggling Goods

CINCINNATI, OHIO, U. S. A.

The Art Printing Co., Cincinnati, O.

Fascimile edition by Moulin & Parole
ISBN: 978-1-958604-22-9

Originally published by Edward Van Wyck, 1900

THE WORLD-RENOWNED KOMEDY KLUB KONJURER,

KOPPE,

IN THE FUNNIEST OF ALL CLUB ACTS.

This is not only a good club act, but also a very funny monologue.

A Real Hot Club act
In which much fun is done
By KOPPE, the
Only One.

Permanent Address, N. Y. Clipper, or any good agent.

THE ORIGINAL CLOWN JUGGLER.

The

Great⁂

Fielding.

If you⁂
want to laugh

WATCH
THE
BOTTLES.

Permanent Address, N. Y. Clipper.

THE CLEVEREST OF THE CLEVER.

C. A. LEEDY.

Baton, Song and Dance, Whistling Solos.

Introducing the quickest and neatest routine of GUN JUGGLING ever presented with a regulation bayoneted musket.

The entire act cleverly arranged into a bright and original single specialty, with every movement set to music.

Permanent Address, N. Y. Clipper.

THE TENNIS TRIO

ALBURTUS,	MILLAR,	HAWLEY,
MORRIS	JESSIE	L. W.

They are the people who deliver the goods in a new and original way. This act pleases the people, is not a quiet act, but always a laughing hit. They use no grease-paint, or props,

ONLY ONE LITTLE INNOCENT
✄✄✄✄BASE BALL MASK✄✄✄✄

Gentlemanly Club Artists Will Not Steal This. Others Must Not.

P. S.—Alburtus, of the Tennis Trio, is the one and only Alburtus, late of Alburtus & Bartram, the originators of double club juggling ten years ago, and were identified with Weber & Fields, Russell Bros., Hyde's Comedians, etc. Also one year in Europe, one season with Tony Pastor; also one year in City of Mexico, Gran Circo Orrin, and now The Tennis Trio, playing the leading theaters and elegant resorts in this country.

Permanent Address, Morris Alburtus, N. Y. Clipper.

THE ARTIST,

MISS JESSIE MILLAR,

Who is creating a big sensation by taking up a line of work which is a vast contrast to her musical talents, and accomplishing the most novel single, double and triple juggling with grace and ease.

P. S. This is the lady that the *San Francisco Call* decorated a whole page with nine different cuts, illustrating her remarkable work with the clubs, while playing the Orpheum with the Tennis Trio.

Address, Morris Alburtus, Tennis Trio, care of N. Y. Clipper.

Comedy Jugglers.

...THE TOSSING AUSTINS...

PLEASING, AMAZING AND FULL OF COMEDY. ❧ DOUBLE TOSSING WITH LAMPS, BALLS, ❧ ❧ ❧ ❧ ❧ UMBRELLAS AND CLUBS.

OUR ORIGINAL COMEDY TRICKS A NOVELTY, AND NEVER FAILS TO MAKE A HIT.

Watch the Dog.

Permanent Address, Victoria Theatre, Dayton, Ohio.

THE GREAT
DARMODY.

Eccentrique Juggling.

❧ ❧

EN ROUTE WITH

....Fads and Follies Co....

❧ ❧

This Act a Laughing Hit.

❧ ❧

Watch the Finish.

Seasons of 1897-98-99

—WITH—

John L. Sullivan's
COMPANY.

❧ ❧

ALWAYS IN IT.

❧ ❧

Permanent   Woburn,
Address,   Mass.

NE PLUS ULTRA OF CLUB ARTISTS.

FRANK L. GREGORY

AN ACT OF GREAT MERIT.

Everything pertaining to this specialty is strictly first class.

U—0—2—C—IT!

PAST SEASONS WITH

Luciers' Minstrels.   San Francisco Minstrel Co.
Boston Star Theater Co.   La Porte Comedy Co.
          This season with Little Trixie Comedy Co.

Permanent Address, New York Clipper, or White Hall, N. Y.

THE VERSATILE DUO.

OHIO **KEHOE** and **RAINER** IDA.

REFINED COMEDY ENTERTAINERS.

SINGERS.

DANCERS.

CLUB
ARTISTS.

DRUM
MAJORS.

First-class dumb act for parks. Up-to-date comedy sketches for theatres.
Also strong "Yankee" comedy sketch, with or without
clubs, entitled "A Fair Mash."

Permanent Address, New York Clipper.

THE PREMIER JUGGLER.

LOUIS

KNETZGER.

Presenting a Novel Original Up - to - Date Specialty.

Introducing original feats of ball tossing, also juggling, swinging, balancing and sliding one, two, three and four clubs.

One of the leading features with Beach & Bowers' Famous Minstrels—season 1899 to 1900.

CLIPPINGS FROM THE PRESS.

In the olio Louis Knetzger is in the lead with some marvelous pyrotechnical club twirling. — *Denver (Col.) Times.*

Louis Knetzger done some juggling feats which made the spectators wonder if they had seen anything like it before. — *Butte (Mont.) Inter-Mountain.*

The juggler, Louis Knetzger, is an expert. His turn is difficult, and yet he does his work without a break or apparent effort. — *Seattle (Wash.) Times.*

Permanent Address, N. Y. Clipper.

THE ORIGINAL HOOP ROLLER.

MASTER EVERHART.

(Old Style 20 Years Ago.)

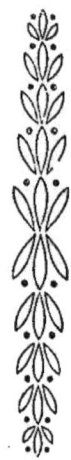

In days gone by this little act was up to the times. Now Mr. Everhart has a Hoop Act that is ahead of the times.

PAST TWO YEARS A CARD WITH AL. G. FIELDS' MINSTRELS.

Year 1900-01 this act will be seen for three months in London, four months in Paris, then a tour of Europe.

See next page for the new style.

THE GREAT EVERHART.

(20 Years Ahead of the Times.)

NOTHING LIKE IT UNDER THE SUN.

Mr. Everhart is the originator of an entirely original act, called HOOP-ROLLING. He has these hoops trained in such a manner that they do the most seemingly impossible feats and tricks with the greatest of ease.

P. S.—Others have attempted this act and failed. They did not buy the right kind of "snake oil," or else they let their hoops stay out too late at night.

THE GREAT
ZIMMER.

America's Droll Juggling Comedian.

SOMEWHAT DIFFERENT FROM THE REST.

This act has played all the leading houses in America. One of the features with Chase & Burke's Big Company.

Permanent Address, N. Y. Clipper.

THE NOVELTY DUO.

Mlle. Brachard...

This lady introduces a clever Juggling Specialty, also a

DRUM MAJOR ACT

—ON A—

ROLLING GLOBE,

And is ably assisted by that great and Remarkable artist,

..Paul Brachard

The most remarkable act of this kind in the world, now one of the features of the Sells-Forepaugh Show.

Permanent Address, New York Clipper.

THE TENNIS DUO.

DOUBLE NOVELTY CLUB JUGGLERS.

ALLAIRE & GAUDRAU.

Have played all the leading Vaudeville houses in America.

Special feature with Culhane, Chase & Weston's Minstrels.

SEASON 1900-1901

VOGEL & DEMING'S BIG MINSTRELS.

Permanent Address, New York Clipper.

PROF. WM. J. HERRMANN,

Physical Instructor
Y. M. C. A.

Fifteenth and Chestnut Sts.
PHILADELPHIA, PA.

❧ ❧

Prof. Herrmann is an expert
with the Clubs.

❧ ❧

SEE NEXT PAGE.

Permanent Address, Y. M. C. A.

H. A. EVEREST,

The Celebrated
High-Class
Club Artist.

❧ ❧

Acknowledged by experts to be
the most artistic Club Swinger
before the public, using in this
act the finest Clubs in the world,
such as musical and other fancy
Clubs.

Permanent Address N. Y. Clipper.

THE ALL-ROUND ATHLETE.

PROF. WM. J. HERRMANN.

Physical Director of Y. M. C. A.
Philadelphia, Pa., Central Branch.

Mr. Herrmann has been the physical director of the Y. M. C. A., Central branch for the past eight years, and is considered by experts to be one of the best all-round athlete, gymnasts, and club artists in America.

Prof. Herrman is an expert in the handling of electric clubs and balls.

Permanent Address, Y. M. C. A., 15th and Chestnut, Philadelphia, Pa.

THE EUROPEAN NOVELTY JUGGLERS.

BROTHERS LISCHKE.

In a very novel and original double club act, doing all the difficult juggling, passing, spinning, and swinging with one, two, three, and four clubs. Many new and original tricks in this act.

Permanent Address, N. Y. Clipper.

ACT OF MIRTH, REFINEMENT, AND ORIGINALITY.

Novel

Artistic

NEWTON.

COMEDY, ACROBATIC CLUB JUGGLER.

A great and sensational juggling act combined with acrobatic and funny situations.

Permanent Address, New York Clipper.

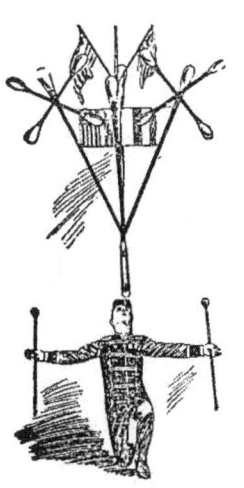

Master Harry Craton

THE CLEVER
AND ARTISTIC

◦ JUGGLER ◦

ON THE SILVER WIRE.

The juggling and wire walking of Master Craton was the best seen here this season.—*Fort Worth Telegram.*

Now en route with Oliver Scott's minstrels.

Permanent Address, N. Y. Clipper.

FRED. SUTHERLAND.

Of Curtis & Sutherland Comedy Company, now en route through
Canada to successful business.

Mr. Sutherland is one of the oldest club-swingers and jugglers now on
the road, and introduces many clever and
novel features in his
act.

Permanent Address, N. Y. Clipper.

THE QUEEN OF CLUBS.

MISS
LA RUE

In a highly artistic specialty of clubs.
Also introducing expert work
with spinning and juggling
batons. New and ele-
gant clubs in
this act.

Permanent   27 Jay St.,
Address,   Cleveland, O.

THE ATHLETIC MARVEL.

Eddie Gillen.

In an act that is novel and different from
the rest.

CLUB JUGGLING
and BAG PUNCHING.

Entire act set to music.

Permanent Address, New York Clipper.

MAJ. KELLIHER.

BATONIST.

Giving an exhibition of fancy and lightning baton swinging. A hit for any band. Special double baton juggling for stage. Now filling dates in New England.

| Permanent Address, | Box 102, Waterbury, Conn. |

EQUILIBRISTIC JUGGLER.

MOSS.

Dexterous Manipulator of Disproportionate Objects.

Originator of Novel and New Ideas in Expert Juggling.

Permanent Address, Hannibal, Mo., or Clipper.

THE NOVELTY ARTIST.

❧ ❧

EDDIE EVANS

❧ ❧

In a clever act with electric clubs. Something entirely new.

THE FLYING VISIONS.

❧ ❧

Also the novel bell clubs.

ROBBERS BE CAREFUL.

Permanent Address,　　　　Edw. Van Wyck, Cincinnati, O.

THE CHAMPION OF PENNSYLVANIA.

DE LONG.

In an entirely new style of club juggling, from one to four clubs.　Also spinning, sliding and passing clubs.　Different from others.

Permanent Address, New York Clipper.

...OUR CLUB CATALOG...

We guarantee you the FINEST Clubs in the world,
And refund your money if misrepresented. ❧ ❧ ❧

No. 1.	No. 2.	No. 3.	No. 4.
2-Club Juggling.	2 and 3-Club Juggling.	3 and 4-Club Juggling.	Double-Club Juggling.

 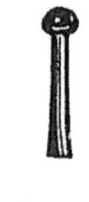   

Length, 2ĭ in.	Length, 20 in.	Length, 19½ in.	Length. 20 in.
Width, 4¾ in.	Width, 4½ in.	Width, 4¼ in.	Width, 4¼ in.
Weight, 19 oz.	Weight, 18 oz.	Weight, 17 oz.	Weight, 18 oz.

The above Clubs, without decorations............each, $1.50.

WE MAKE ANYTHING IN THE LINE OF CLUBS.

Juggling Clubs have our new improved Hardwood handles, Ebony or Cherry finish, are White Enameled, Rubber attachments for bottoms—"our invention." These Clubs are decorated in Electric Red, Green, Gold or Silver, Plain or Hammer style. We are also the inventors of this style of decorating................ .... Per Club, **$2.50 to $3.00**

Swinging Clubs—19 in. long; weight, 14 to 16 oz., Ebony finish, decorated to give them the Electric Light effect.
Per Pair......... . ... **$4.50 to $6.00**

Balancing Club for one-club work, and for spinning and sliding. Made like a Juggling Club. 21 in. long, 4¾ in. wide, 20 oz.. .... **$3.00**

We make a specialty of Novelty Clubs, such as Electric Clubs, Musical, Bounding and Bell Clubs, also South American Bolos —our own invention.

➤——PRICES ON APPLICATION.——◄

We are the inventors of all the latest improvements on goods of this kind. When you buy, buy of us, and you get the latest and THE BEST.

TERMS—One-third Cash, balance C. O. D.

EDWARD VAN WYCK, Cincinnati, Ohio, U. S. A.